A COACHING STORY

Using Coaching to Manage your Company

How to Use the Infinite Power of Change to Achieve your Corporate Goals

Carlos Ballerino Moeller

Editing
Ralph Dexter

Cover and Graphics
Gustavo Silva Guerrero "Japi"

A COACHING SPTORY

Using Coaching to Manage your Company

How to Use the Infinite Power of Change to Achieve your Corporate Goals

Author: Carlos Ballerino Moeller

Published by; Carlos Ballerino Moeller

To God, who gave me life.

To my daughter Sofia Ballerino Leigh, your love awakens in me each day the will to overcome

To my parents, Carlos Ballerino and Ilse Moeller, who strived to give me love and teach me the things that are truly important in life.

To my children who left their mark on this beautiful earth, Fiorella, my angel who was not able to come into this world; Charlie and Camila Ballerino Leigh, who are examples of the irrepressible force of the human spirit. Thank you for helping me see things from the best possible standpoint –everyday happiness! For the love you gave me that filled my whole life. For your strength in the face of pain that helped me endure adversity. For your passage to a better life that gave me the best of gifts – to live each day as if it were my last, give my all each day and reflect on all life's experiences.

To my siblings, Andrés, Teresa, Jorge and Fernando Ballerino, for their constant support at all stages of my life.

To my dear sister-in-law, Dr. Sonia María Escobar Viteri, by means of whose excellent nutritional prescriptions and follow up I was able to restore my health, one of the most important aspects of life.

To my dear nieces and nephews, my dear godson, Andrés Gonzalo, Teresa and her little Alvarito, Maria José, Eliana and Andreita, for their constant desire to learn.

To all my relatives, uncles, aunts and cousins, who have always been there for me.

To my friends, for their tenderness, patience, wise advice, and especially for their love.

To everyone who contributed in one way or another to my continuous learning in this wonderful life.

TABLE OF CONTENTS

If you treat **people**
as you find them,
you will make them worse;
if you treat them
as they could be,
you will make them better.

Johann Wolfgang Von Goethe

This is a modern story that can and should be applied every day in one's life, in one's family, and in one's work; in other words, it should become a day-to-day living experience.

It is an invitation to reflect on a new path that could become a unique opportunity…

I

THE ENCOUNTER

Andrew Oak, a distinguished and successful executive, was walking alone on a major avenue. The city was just beginning to wake up as the dawn began to shed its light. Wrapped in the silence of the morning, he entered an almost deserted coffee shop and saw a young man seated nearby. He was reading a book that was familiar to him. Cautiously and somewhat intrigued, he approached the young man and asked him why he had chosen that author.

-Do you like Drucker?- he finally asked.

-I really don't know… But his ideas intrigue me, and his eloquence surprises me. In so few words he is able to portray all the intrigue of the universe, so much so that the words whirl around my head and cause me to question the true meaning of life- explained the young man. – I will read you a sentence – he said, concentrating once again on the book: "Management always deals with the nature of man, and with good and evil."

The quote was followed by the exchange of opinions on the contents of the book. In the middle of this fascinating conversation, Andrew stopped, and turning to the young man, exclaimed:

-You haven't told me your name, or your story. Tell me a bit about yourself.

-My name is Charles Louis – my friends call me Charlie. I just graduated from the university in Business Administration, and am currently looking for work, a job where I can achieve my full potential as a human being and also learn more about being a manager.

-An interesting quest! – exclaimed Andrew, impressed by the profound response.

-But do you think that kind of company exists? Do you think you could find a job like that? How do you plan to achieve those dreams?

-I still can't figure out or describe exactly what I am looking for: a magic formula that would inextricably combine the objective world of a company with the subjectivity of the essence of a human being – explained Charlie -. I only know that I am looking for dreams; that dimension where there is life and something you have to believe in. I am looking for the magic of men and women, and that inner voice … The foolishness of a youth starting life full of hopes and ideals!

-Do you know what, Charlie?– Andrew confessed. To a certain extent, I can see myself in your search. It is a lesson that requires a bit of imagination, a bit of foolishness, but especially humility. Einstein said:

**"The more I learn, the more I realize
I don't know,
and the more I realize I don't know,
the more I want to learn.
In the middle of difficulty
is opportunity.
I think and think for months and years.
Ninety-nine times the conclusion is false,
The hundredth time I am right.
With deep reflection from daily life
one knows that one exists for other people.
The important thing is not to stop questioning yourself."**

-A fantastic thought! I hadn't heard it before, although I love Einstein's philosophy, answered Charlie.

-Well, it has affected a lot of things in my life, added Andrew.

Noting that the time had passed quickly, Andrew explained that he had to head for his office because there were unavoidable obligations that needed his attention. However, he asked Charlie to accompany him during the walk to his office, which was a few blocks from the coffee shop where they had met. That would give them a bit more time to continue sharing interests and thoughts on life.
Finally they arrived outside a very large, beautiful building with panoramic elevators and luxurious finishes.

-Look at this building, Charlie,- said Andrew.

-It's impressive! I would love to work in a place like this. The offices must be very comfortable and have modern equipment – exclaimed Charlie.

-Yes, it is a very beautiful building- commented Andrew-. However, that's not the most important thing. As we were saying before, what's really valuable is trained human talent. Confucius said:

"Success depends on previous preparation, and without such previous preparation there is sure to be failure."

-This is obviously a company that took a lot of planning; at least that's what it looks like from the outside- said Charlie, a bit doubtful.

Noting this, Andrew continued:
-For it to be like that inside the organization, there are several prerequisites, including the planning you mentioned. You have to visualize what you are going to do. It is very important to remember that this visualization includes a very interesting method called modeling excellence, which is only applied consistently by companies that are market leaders. That is, they take as a model the successful processes of other companies that are not necessarily in the same field, and adapt them to their business, their leadership style, and their way of doing things. So on one hand, they have the best of the best, and on the other, the best of themselves.

You should also know the importance of discernment; that is, choosing what is always a priority in your planning and your process, in other words, knowing how to choose from the whole what you should do first, then second, third, and so forth. When you do this, you are organizing your business correctly. You should give a lot of importance to working only with what you need, because everything you don't need will result in an unnecessary expense of time and resources that serve only to slow you down without you realizing it. With these tools as well as excellent personal wellbeing and self-discipline, you will undoubtedly achieve all the objectives you set for yourself.

-Excellent explanation- commented Charlie, very interested in his new friend.

II

THE DIRECTOR

Standing in front of the door to the fabulous building and still digesting Andrew's final comments, Charlie decided to ask:

-We have stopped in front of this building… does that mean that this is your office?

-That is correct,- replied Andrew. This is one of my offices.

-One of them? – asked Charlie.

The thing is, along the way I have generated employment and, of course, several companies. This is one of them. You know- continued Andrew, -I liked the way you expressed yourself during our conversation. You must also be good in action.

-Why do you say that? Are you going to offer me a job?- asked Charlie jokingly.

-Well, yes.- answered Andrew. I am a businessman with a good eye for choosing managers. I use my intelligence and my feelings wisely, and I have seen in you what it takes for top management.

-But you hardly know me– exclaimed Charlie a bit nervously. -How do you know I will be able to deal with major challenges, like managing one of your successful companies?

-I know you will do a good job. I trust you and my experience discovering human talent,– explained Andrew.- Besides, you will have four assistant managers beside you to manage the most important areas of the company. They will be your subordinates. With the right decisions and delegation, they will ensure that the company achieves the desired results. You'll see!

OK! – replied Carlos, as he remembered something his grandmother used to say to him when he was a child: **"It is always better to have an option than not to have any."** This as an opportunity for personal growth,- declared Charlie.- Thank you. I accept!

III

THE FOUR ASSISTANT MANAGERS

Charlie went into the main office of the building. Andrew told him he would be working there, and in fact, there was his luxurious oak desk with several things needing to be dispatched. He sat down and began studying the information that was in front of him. Although he spent the whole day working, the situation of the company was still perplexing. Night was falling when he remembered that Andrew had told him he would have four collaborators. He saw an intercom nearby and used it immediately.

He called many times until a man finally appeared at the door.

-Good afternoon- said Charlie.

The man entered the office with a lighted cigar in his mouth and a white hat on his head. Arrogantly and without returning the greeting, he exclaimed in a questioning tone:

-So you're the new Director General?

Charlie, while waiting for his greeting to be returned, remembered his mother's advice:

"Always be courteous and fair, regardless of how others treat you. Don't let them determine your response."

Yes,- answered Charlie. I didn't hear your name when you came in. What is it?

-That was because I didn't tell you- the man answered arrogantly. My name is Edward Mind. I am the most important person in the company. I handle absolutely everything. I have control. I am better than everybody else who works here, but that shouldn't interest you right now, but rather how the company is doing.

-Yes, that's right – agreed Charlie. I was looking at these papers and I find them perplexing and very much in disarray. I can't figure them out.

-That is because the company is about to go bankrupt – answered Mind. Alarmed, Charlie countered:

-What? It's about to what?

-Go bankrupt! Just like you heard big shot!- replied Mind, treating Charlie without respect and ignoring his position. Don't tell me our President didn't say anything to you?- he asked insidiously. The company is in financial trouble. We have a deficit, lots of accounts receivable, and we are producing at less than half our installed capacity.

-Andrew didn't tell me anything about this. He was honest and sincere with me.- Charlie said to himself. I don't understand why he appointed me manager if the company is bankrupt.

-Yes. Why did he appoint you?- scoffed Mind. I suppose he had you sign a contract, right?

-Yes– replied Charlie, nodding his head.

-Did you notice the date?- asked Mind maliciously.

-No– Charlie answered. I didn't notice. It happened very quickly. He had the contract in his briefcase. I signed it as soon as he gave it to me and returned it to him immediately.

-Well, the date on that contract is a year ago, precisely when the company started to go down, and now you will be the one responsible. You will bear the full weight of the law.

-That can't be!- exclaimed Charlie. Andrew wouldn't do that to me.

-Why not! Didn't you say that you two had just met?– stressed Mind.

-Yes, but he told me he was a successful businessman and that he had lots of companies.

-Yes, that's correct. He has lots of companies.- replied Mind as he approached the balcony. Do you see that building across the street?

-The one where there seems to be a celebration on the top floor, and they are shooting off fireworks? – asked Charlie.

-Yes, that one.- answered Mind. That is another of Andrew's companies. It had a good year and fantastic profits. I wonder why didn't he give you that company to manage?- he added sarcastically.

Mind then walked out of the office, leaving Charlie worried, stressed, and full of doubts. Very concerned, he began analyzing everything his subordinate had said. Was it true? Had he fallen into a trap? He decided to keep investigating and pressed the second button on the intercom.

After a few minutes, a person appeared who made fruitless efforts to enter the office. His size and portliness prevented him from doing so. With great effort, the obese figure managed to come in. In his hands he had a sandwich, a pizza, and ice cream that he was trying to eat all at once, while juggling them to keep any of his treats from falling.

-What's your name? – asked Charlie.

-I'm Peter Body – the man answered, almost choking on a pepperoni. I am in charge of the systems structure of the organization.

-You mean the systems department manager?- asked Charlie.

-That's right- answered Body, without being able to stop eating.

Sir, I know you are here to manage this company,- he said shakily, demonstrating his low self-esteem and shyness.- But you don't know what a mess you've gotten yourself into. This company is very slow in my area; the equipment and technology are obsolete. Nothing has been upgraded. The previous manager used to tell us that is was an unnecessary expense. I told him that it was a strategic investment to beat our competition,- he added, almost pleadingly,- but he paid no attention to me, and I began to get worried and depressed. I tried to do something with what I had, but things got worse and worse until finally all the equipment was obsolete, and these are our work tools. You have no idea how hard it is to make the systems work to satisfy the few customers we have left! I am worn out from everything that's happening. I tire very quickly, and I don't know what to do to remedy the situation,- he confessed as he left the office almost in tears.

Charlie was very concerned after listening to Body, and began to think that it had been a bad bargain to meet Andrew. In desperation, he pressed another button on the intercom. The third collaborator appeared. He came in talking before Charlie could ask him anything.

-So you are Charlie – he said angrily.

-That is correct.

-Well, I'm Alberto Memories, and I think you are very unlucky to be here. I am going to tell you about the worst things that have happened to you in the past. Perhaps that exam when you were nervous and got a bad grade, or all the times you tripped or fell down, hurting yourself because you weren't careful. Maybe that business deal you thought about making some time ago, but abandoned because you convinced yourself that you were a failure. Or better yet, remember when things started to go wrong and you dropped everything. That lead you to look for a job and you ended up here in this failing business that only a miracle could save- said the man, ending his devastating narration.- Don't forget that your memories of the past are the only thing you have to worry about. As far as I'm concerned, they have all been catastrophic. I wish you luck in your attempt because you're going to need it.- he added with obvious pessimism as he left the office.

Charlie' doubts and anxiety only increased after such pathetic words. -What should he do?- he thought as he poured himself some coffee. The caffeine only made him more upset. -Everything's falling apart,- he thought. What did I do to deserve this? Who should he turn to? Well, I have one more subordinate to call. Perhaps he will be the solution, he thought hopefully as he pressed the last button on the intercom.

A thin, trembling man appeared. Stuttering, he introduced himself:

-Ha... ha... hello. Ma... ma... my name is Joe Feelings and I have spoken to all my colleagues. Like them I ba... ba... believe that you are ga... ga... getting into a very da... da... deep hole, difficult to get out of. All the... the... the staff is very nervous; they have la... la... little faith that the company will recover. We are also behind in paying the salaries, and... and... and a union is being organized to protect their interests. Th... th... they want to organize a strike. E... e... everybody is very angry because the pa... pa... promises the previous manager made to them have not been kept, and they think that this is going ba... ba... belly up. They are afraid th... th... they are going to lose their jobs. They are very discouraged and sad about the situation because ma... ma... many have families and they don't know what they will do if they lose their jobs. The sa... sa... suppliers call and call about their payments, and they are about to take us to court. You have no idea how the company is doing. I am va... va... very concerned. I can't think and my colleagues don't help me. On the contrary, they are making me more and more nervous. There is no team work and na... na... nobody motivates us. There is no pa... pa... planning, no goals, nothing. We're da... da... desperate.

As he said these final words, Feelings was almost in tears; he ran to the door, went out, and disappeared into the dark corridor.

This can't be, I feel cheated, thought Charlie. From the outside, it looked like a well-organized enterprise. I thought motivated people would be working here with strategies and clear goals to guide them and their work. Why didn't Andrew tell me about any of this? Did he want to set a trap for me so that there would be somebody to take the responsibility for this disaster, and then blame me so that I would have to face the courts. I feel really paralyzed after so much bad news and I am afraid of what might happen…

After sitting for hours at his desk in his European leather chair, thinking and thinking, reviewing and looking at papers, studying historical records and emails from past administrations, and going around and around in circles, he thought: The only solution is to go to Andrew and confront him to see what is really happening and why he put me in charge of this company.

IV

WHEN THE STUDENT IS READY, THE TEACHER SHARES WISDOM

When he saw the headquarters of the consortium Andrew managed, Charlie was impressed. The building was sober and elegant, but not extravagant. When he entered Andrew's office, he noticed that it contained the bare minimum.

-I don't understand- said Charlie. How is it that you have such modern, functional buildings, but the place where you work is so simple and has only the essentials?

-My dear Charlie, in this life you only need the essentials, because we are here today, and tomorrow perhaps not- Andrew replied.

-But how sad to think that we could die tomorrow!- exclaimed Charlie.

-Dying is not sad my dear friend. The sad thing is that most people never live. And as far as modern buildings are concerned, I try to ensure that my collaborators always have the best, because I am here to serve them. Moreover, I believe I should provide them with the best tools, support their knowledge, and motivate them constantly to nurture a positive attitude, so that they can fulfill with excellence the mission entrusted to them and become a successful team.

-By the way,- Charlie interrupted angrily- How is it that you sent me to a company that is collapsing financially and can't even pay the basic things to stay in operation?- None of what you just mentioned happens there; moreover, the subordinates you put me in charge of told me that I signed a backdated contract with you, and now I'm in big trouble.

Andrew remained calm despite Charlie's vehemence and despair. With a conciliatory smile he began to instruct him in a wise manner:

-My dear Charlie,- he said, here is your contract. Please review it. I clearly remember that you signed it quickly and didn't even take the precaution of keeping a copy. However, do you see anything you don't like?

Charlie began to read the document nervously from the back to the front, because the last page contained the date. Glancing at it he realized it was today's date, and not months earlier, as Mind had suggested. He then began to calm down. As he went over it carefully, he realized that it was exceptional, because it contained clauses that would allow him to become a shareholder in the company if he fulfilled certain guidelines and goals, and then serve on the Board of Directors of Andrew's business conglomerate and receive a share package. But he was even more surprised to see that the contract specified that if the company had financial problems, the conglomerate would support him economically until it recovered or had to be liquidated, and that the manager could resign without detriment whenever he wished.

Charlie couldn't imagine that anybody could be so generous. -But why did he put me in the worst company in the conglomerate?- Charlie thought. Suddenly he found himself saying:

-All this is incredible Andrew, and the truth is I trusted you so much I didn't even read the contract.

Andrew interrupted him, -And what did you learn from this experience?

-That I should always read important documents to find out what is most advantageous- answered Charlie.

-Excellent reflection- noted Andrew.

-Remember, continued Andrew:

The problems you encounter in life are simply situations that lead to results, undesirable in some cases and desirable in others, but they're still only situations. If you can view them like that, you will always learn something positive from them, and they will become a key part of your learning and growth.

There is always a way to resolve situations. If you take time to reflect and find a way to extricate yourself from the cause, rather than just worrying, you will become a Master.

Noting that Andrew had fallen silent, Charlie resumed the conversation.

-As I was saying, it all seems marvelous and I'm grateful, but there's something I don't understand. Why did you put me in the company that has the most problems and is about to go bankrupt, when there is another one across the street that's shooting off fireworks to celebrate its profits?

Once again smiling graciously, Andrew explained:

-I should tell you, my dear friend, that the company you just mentioned is celebrating the successful achievement of its goals. Two years ago it reported much bigger losses than the ones you have under your nose right now, and if I hadn't found someone so intelligent, honest, hard-working, empowering and well-organized, I would have had to close it down. That person is heading the organization you saw, and he has a contract very similar to the one you have in your hands. He got the company off the ground so well that they ended the year with the highest profits in the conglomerate. The fireworks were to celebrate the sharing of the profits, because I promised that if they achieved their goal, I would distribute half the earnings of the conglomerate among all the collaborators. That was the reason for the fireworks. They were simply celebrating their prosperity. **They understand clearly that anyone who tries to obtain prosperity only for themselves ends up in poverty; but those who consider the whole world their home, and truly care and strive to achieve abundance and prosperity for their collaborators, the world, and their company, achieve personal prosperity that nobody will take from them.**

Charlie was astonished by the success story of the company across the street. He was silent for a long time thinking: Why didn't I ask or find out about this? Why did I simply believe the gossip of my subordinates? From now on I will keep this phrase in my mind:

"I will never assume, I will always inquire."

-Now I see a new question in your mind. Why did you give me collaborators who complain so much? Right?- asked Andrew.

Astonished at the perception of his boss, Charlie nodded his head.

-Well, I can tell you that each was chosen for his excellent resume and ample experience. However, we have detected a problem that was like a virus created by the previous administration,- said Andrew.

-A virus?- asked Charlie.

-Yes, a virus like one that can be caught by a person and almost kill him, or by a computer and erase valuable information or damage the operating system- Andrew explained.

-What are these viruses?- asked Charlie, concerned and anxious to obtain lots of information from a guru like Andrew, so he could capitalize on it and get started.

-This virus has to do with beliefs- said Andrew.

-Beliefs?- Charlie interjected doubtfully.

-Yes, beliefs- emphasized Andrew.

V

BELIEFS THAT PARALYZE

-Beliefs can be as bad as viruses, and they hold you back you when you try to achieve something- explained Andrew. There are people who hang on to an idea. They always got the expected results doing things the same way they did before, so they think the information invariably has to be correct. Then, when someone comes with new information, they don't accept it because their ego doesn't allow them see that it could be more useful to them and to the organization.

-I don't understand- said Charlie.

Andrew answered patiently: I will explain using a historical example:

In the 60's, Switzerland dominated the watch industry. Their excellence had been recognized for more than a century. In 1968, they had 65% of the world market and 80% profit. However, a decade later, their market share had fallen to less than 10%, and in the next three years they had to fire 50,000 of the 60,000 workers in the industry. What do you think caused this drastic loss of market share?- asked Andrew.

-I don't know. Tell me- asked Charlie.

-It was because they stuck to the belief that watches would always be manufactured in the same way. And who do you think took advantage of this limiting belief of the Swiss, which prevented them from seeing beyond their own noses?

Who? Who?- asked Charlie insistently.

-Japan- replied Andrew. They had no limiting beliefs. On the contrary, they took advantage of the new ideas that were appearing at that time, and launched a quartz watch on the world market. Totally electronic watches, a thousand times more accurate than mechanical, battery-operated watches. What a brilliant idea! Right?

-Yes. What an impressive story, and what an expansive belief the Japanese had!- noted Charlie.

-And do you know who came up with that marvelous idea- asked Andrew.

-No. I don't know. Who?- asked Charlie.

-Well, believe it or not, the quartz watch was invented by the Swiss themselves in their own laboratories in Meuchatel.- explained Andrew. However, when the researchers presented the idea to the manufacturers in 1967, they rejected it outright because there were no bearings, gears or even springs. This could not be the future of watches. So confident were they in their conclusions that they didn't even bother to protect the idea. That same year, the researchers showed the new watch to the world at the annual watch manufacturers' conference. Texas Instruments from United States and Seiko from Japan came by, and looked, and the rest is history. Now, why do you think the Swiss didn't appreciate this fantastic idea that their own people had created?

-I think they were blind- Charlie suggested.

-Correct. They allowed themselves to be trapped by a limiting belief that was full of old ways of doing things and triumphs from the past. It did not allow them to see that a new idea was being born. They didn't develop the art of always working with the expansive beliefs that change the world. They didn't understand that even if they didn't agree with them, the world and its ideas would continue on their way and nothing could stop them- said Andrew. They were definitely unable to see the future. They were blinded by ego, and they thought that no one else could do things right or differently from their way, and that caused their fall. This new idea simply did not fit the rules they were used to. This story as a good example and always remember that what was successful in the past will not necessarily be successful in the future.

Your past does not guarantee anything in the future if the rules change.

"Even the best watchmakers of the world cannot stop time"

-In fact, if you are not careful your successful past can impede your vision of the future, and that is why you should be open to new ideas, and full of expansive beliefs that will allow you to explore different ways of doing things.- said Andrew. That is the belief I apply in my daily life as a businessman:

"My company and my products can be reinvented continuously, as many times as necessary, and the only things that are capable of influencing change are our creativity, our attitudes, technology, and most importantly, our customers."

-It is incredible that limiting beliefs can prevent you from seeing that there are other possibilities, and this happens in all areas of our lives. That is why I am going to tell you about an experience from my personal life- confessed Andrew. When I was 12, I had an infection in my hip that was so bad I almost died. It was caused by a virus that destroyed the cartilage. Despite my young age, I had to have an operation, and the doctors fused my femur to the rest of the bones of my hip. As a result, I could not move my left hip. I had been very active, but now the doctors ordered me to abandon almost all sports. This had a big effect on me, and I was convinced that I would never again be able to participate in sports or martial arts, which I loved. Moreover, it had been one of my goals to learn Karate, and because of this problem, my dream would be thwarted forever.

-What has that got to do with limiting beliefs?- interjected Charlie.

-Be patient- replied Andrew calmly.

VI

BELIEFS THAT PRODUCE CHANGE

-You will have noticed that I always like to attend seminars and conferences, and even study other careers. Right?- asked Andrew.

Charlie nodded his head in agreement.

-A few years ago, before I started my companies, I enrolled in a Management Skills Training Program. I was surprised that a lot of time and effort was dedicated to the human aspect of each of us. That was when I heard about limiting beliefs and how to tell if you have any,- Andrew continued.

-OK, but how does this relate to karate?- asked Charlie expectantly.

-One day I realized that I had this mental block because of what the doctors told me, and I hadn't even thought about asking what I could do,- explained Andrew. I was even more surprised when I broke the barrier created by that limiting belief. Life taught me how important it is to be aware of this virus. I went and asked a friend with a black belt in karate who had known me for a long time whether I could learn that martial art, and do you know what he told me?-

-What did he tell you?- replied Charlie, intrigued

-He said yes, I could!- said Andrew, deeply moved. Despite my handicap I could learn. He also told me that the Sensei would value me for what I could do, not for what I couldn't do, and that his type of karate didn't require continuous physical contact. It was more an art of learning in Katas, and the karatekas took care of each other like a brotherhood. So I immediately began practicing it and I have been involved in it for some time. I managed to turn my limiting belief into an extensive one.

-That story is incredible!- exclaimed Charlie. We can have mental blocks without even knowing it!

-Yes. The mind often plays dirty tricks on us, if we let it. That's why it is important to be calm,- said Andrew, quoting one of his favorite sayings:

When the mind is calm, life is perceived with great clarity and beauty.

-I could give you more examples- continued Andrew. I had a friend who always said that he was stupid when it came to English. It goes without saying that every time he said that, the virus got into his head and his mind processed it to make sure that he never learned English. One day I told him about limiting beliefs and how they harm our personality and prevent us from advancing and being happy. He was interested, so we did the exercise. The first thing was to find an institute that suited his budget. He enrolled and of course he found the language difficult, but despite that, he managed to graduate.

-That's great! He was able to transform his beliefs- exclaimed Charlie enthusiastically.

-Not only that- added Andrew. He also noticed that his companions who found the language easy dropped out or put it off until later, saying that they could learn it "anytime." They never graduated.

-It's incredible that so much talent is wasted!- declared Charlie.

-You said it- Andrew acknowledged. As you can see, the problem with your subordinates is that they have filled themselves with this virus of limiting beliefs due to the mental block the previous administration created. And they want to pass it to you too, without malice of course, by only giving you negative information, and making you relive tragic memories and feel frustrated, and giving you superficial feedback, as if they weren't responsible for what's happening. The previous manager's ego was so large he couldn't see what was happening, so he quit. I wanted to help him get the company going with new information, but he refused to accept my help. He refused to listen to the messages.

-What do you mean when you say he refused to listen to the messages?- asked Charlie.

Then Andrew told him a story to explain it better.

-A man was walking down a path- Andrew began. He hadn't gone very far when he suddenly met a camel. Incredibly, the animal spoke to him and warned him: "Don't continue on this path. There are some thieves up ahead and they can harm you." "What is this?" the man exclaimed, amazed that a camel had spoken and by the message it had given him. -I must be losing my mind,- he thought. -Why shouldn't I continue on this path? The other is much longer and takes too much skill, because you have to climb a couple of very steep mountains!- Ignoring the message he continued on the path he had chosen originally. After walking a few hours a group of criminals caught up to him and threatened him with sabers. They beat him severely and took everything he had. Half dead, he was rescued by a villager who was passing by. He helped him up, took him to his home, and called a doctor to treat him. A week later after he had recovered, he continued on his way, and met the camel again. Ashamed and free of prejudice now, he told the camel how unhappy and sorry he was that he had not followed his suggestion to take a different route. The camel replied: **"Messages only come when you need them. If you dare to listen to them wisely, they will be useful. Otherwise they will act against you."**

-I hope I have the wisdom to identify the messages I get and am able to listen to them- Charlie exclaimed.

-Yes indeed- replied Andrew:

Ego can blind you to the possibilities.

-There is something you really need to be understand, Charlie- Andrew continued. You have to visualize that these collaborators of yours are your subordinates. They are there to obey your orders, and not the other way around. You should orient and guide them, and make a team out of them. Develop a strategic plan for getting out of the debacle that the company is in.

VII

THE FORMULA

-Do you really believe the company can be saved?- asked Charlie incredulously.

-I not only believe it, my dear friend, I'm sure of it- declared Andrew.

-And what's the formula for accomplishing that?- Charlie asked.

-Do you remember our conversation in the coffee shop? Andrew countered.

-How could I forget is!- exclaimed Charlie.

-Well, that conversation is part of the formula. Now you need to put into practice all the things that impressed me about you, all the positive experiences, and all the mechanisms required to implement and manage.

Remember that knowledge is simply disorganized information. Wisdom lies in organizing that information and putting it into practice.

This is the formula: $C \times A = R$

KNOWLEDGE X ACTION = RESULTS
Knowledge multiplied by Action will produce the desired results with which we will achieve the hoped for change.

Knowledge is information. Action gives us information. So all events are positive if we see them like this:

"Failure does not exist; everything is feedback and feedback is only information."

Remember that failure as such does not exist, only situations in which we sometimes do not achieve the desired results. These situations result in learning and feedback, and we should obtain the necessary information from these experiences to persevere and achieve the hoped for results, and also learn from them so we can replicate them successfully.

VIII

THE LADDER OF SUCCESS

-Bear in mind- began Andrew that you have to prepare the soil before you can plant. That preparation is planning, and you have to add a tool that I always use because it's so simple:

The Ladder of Success

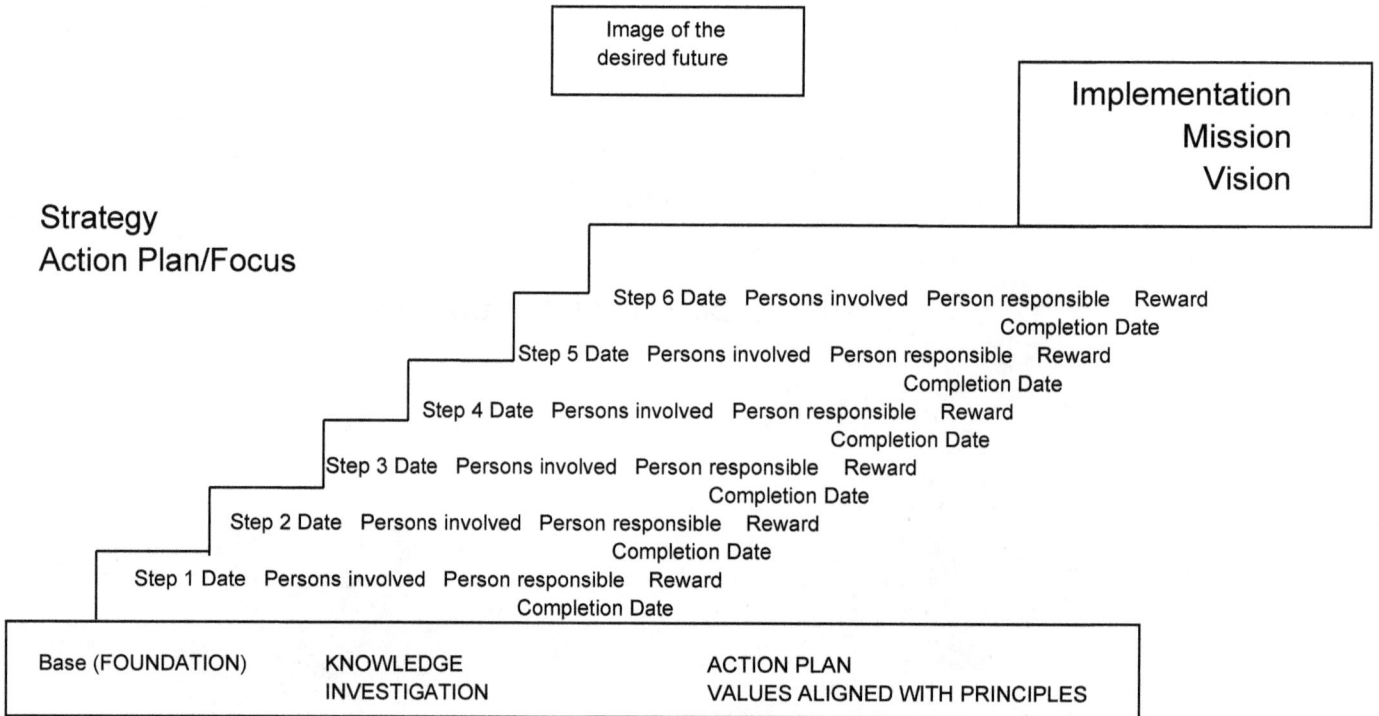

Image of the desired future

Implementation
Mission
Vision

Strategy
Action Plan/Focus

Step 6 Date   Persons involved   Person responsible   Reward
                                              Completion Date

Step 5 Date   Persons involved   Person responsible   Reward
                                              Completion Date

Step 4 Date   Persons involved   Person responsible   Reward
                                              Completion Date

Step 3 Date   Persons involved   Person responsible   Reward
                                              Completion Date

Step 2 Date   Persons involved   Person responsible   Reward
                                              Completion Date

Step 1 Date   Persons involved   Person responsible   Reward
                                              Completion Date

Base (FOUNDATION)	KNOWLEDGE INVESTIGATION	ACTION PLAN VALUES ALIGNED WITH PRINCIPLES

29

The Ladder of Success.

**CONTINUAL IMPROVEMENT = CONTINUAL
FULFILLMENT OF THE MISSION AND VISION**

-You were already prepared to succeed- continued Andrew- but your limiting beliefs caused a mental block and made you think you couldn't. However, right now you and I are going to trace the ladder that will achieve the goal that you are going to choose for yourself. This is the last tool I'm going to give you for the time being.

-Why a ladder?- asked Charlie.

-Why not?- replied Andrew, to make Charlie think.

Then he explained:

-A ladder shows us the gradual ascent to what we want to achieve. It also shows us each of the rungs we have to climb in order to reach our destination. On each of these rungs you have to put the dates by which we will fulfill what we have proposed, and when we fulfill them, we will reward ourselves with something simple, such as ice cream. That encourages us to keep climbing and advancing until the moment arrives when, without even realizing it, we reach the top. In this way, the ascent is easier despite day-to-day difficulties.

We can model excellence, even genius, if we divide tasks into small enough sections. If somebody can so something, then it is humanly possible that anything can be achieved.

-What a great idea and how wise those ideas are!- exclaimed Charlie.

Andrew continued:

-Now I'm going to show you what each rung of that wise ladder consists of...

VIII

IMPLEMENTATION

First you have to be very clear about your vision, that is, your image of the desired future, where you want to be after a certain amount of time. For example, it might be that you want to get a Master's Degree in Business Administration. The vision then would be to get an MBA in two years. In the case of a company, to be recognized as an organization with commitment, professionalism, quality, competitive costs, and a high rate of satisfaction in Customer Service, after 5 years.

After defining the vision, you should continue underpinning the foundations, which are the basis of all planning. This point requires a lot of investigation and knowledge of everything that is to be achieved. Using the same examples, you would have to investigate which university best suits your time and budget, and under this point you would have to include several alternatives in order to have a wider range of choices. In the case of the company, you would have to do market research on the needs of your customers, and how they can be satisfied, what the competition offers them and what it does not, so that when the new company offers it, it can cause a change the market in your favor in your favor.

After choosing the points you will cover in your research, you should start drawing each rung of the ladder. Remember that each of them is very important because it will provide you with the necessary satisfaction to go after the next success. Always remember this phrase:

Enjoyment of the trip is what provides true happiness, much more than the destination itself.

You should put the goal you want to achieve on each rung. It is a mini goal that will help you feel that you are accomplishing an important part of your final objective. If we use the example of the Master's Degree again, the initial objective would be to complete the first year by the agreed date. It is the same with the company. Specify the persons involved by area, who will do what, when, and how it is going to be measured to be able to control the process. Each rung is a step toward success. But remember that:

Never lose focus. You need to be like a race horse that has visualized the goal and doesn't rest until it has been reached.

While Andrew was explaining, Charlie took out his planner and began drawing his own ladder.

Charlie's Ladder of Success

Vision: To be recognized as an organization that produces with commitment, professionalism, quality, competitive costs, and a high rate of satisfaction in Customer Service.

The Ladder of Success

I am a successful General Manager

Implementation Date
Month, Day, Year

Strategy
To create daily commitment

Action Plan: To create a suitable environment for company employees.
Focus: I am a successful General Manager

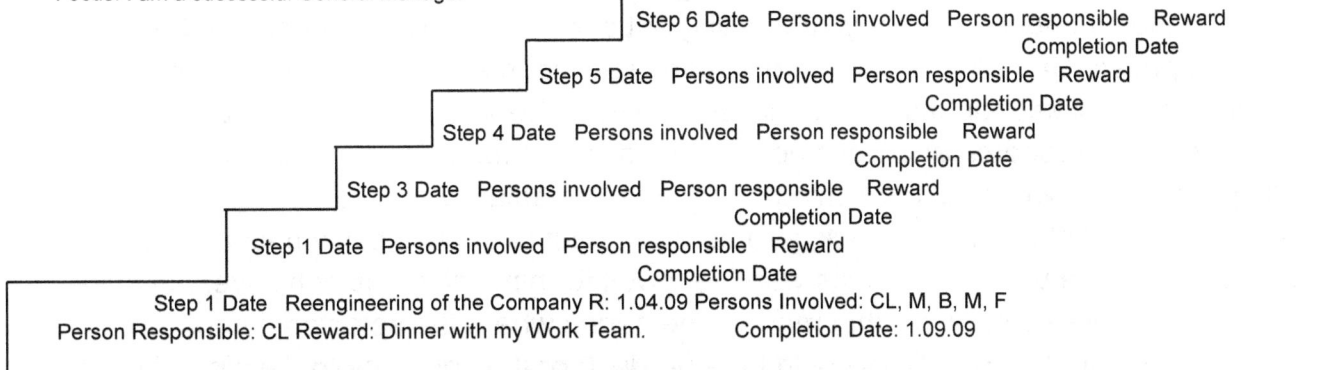

Step 6 Date   Persons involved   Person responsible   Reward
Completion Date

Step 5 Date   Persons involved   Person responsible   Reward
Completion Date

Step 4 Date   Persons involved   Person responsible   Reward
Completion Date

Step 3 Date   Persons involved   Person responsible   Reward
Completion Date

Step 1 Date   Persons involved   Person responsible   Reward
Completion Date

Step 1 Date   Reengineering of the Company R: 1.04.09 Persons Involved: CL, M, B, M, F
Person Responsible: CL Reward: Dinner with my Work Team.   Completion Date: 1.09.09

Base (FOUNDATION) KNOWLEDGE:
Investigate the different types of tools
my subordinates require.

ACTION PLAN:
INVESTIGATION: Investigate the principal
motivations and skills of my collaborators.

VALUES ALIGNED WITH PRINCIPLES
Page: 42

Remember that you should always have a strategy and be prepared for any contingency or situation that comes between you and your goal. You should know that the person with the greatest flexibility in any situation will be more influential and will be able to achieve greater success. This means that if you started by studying Commercial Engineering and during your career you had to switch to Marketing, which will definitely be the right career. It is the same with the company. If the market undergoes a sudden change, your directors should be sufficiently flexible to change with it.

-I will tell you about a very big company, 3M- said Andrew. I am sure you have heard of it.

-Of course- replied Charlie, paying close attention to the entire explanation. –Please tell me about it.

-Do you know that 3M used to be called Minnesota Mining & Manufacturing Co. It was a very old company in United States. It was founded in 1902, and was exclusively involved in manufacturing machinery for mining. However, the years went by and after serious economic crises and fluctuations in the market, it had to change. At that time one of the employees was a member of a church choir, and he was having trouble marking the hymns he was supposed to sing. He used pieces of paper to separate the pages of the hymnbook, but they kept falling out and making him lose track of the selected pages. One Monday after the Sunday service, tired of what was always happening, he asked for help from a fellow-worker who was in charge of the Department of Research and Development. As soon as he got to his office he started telling him about what was happening. His friend immediately replied that he had a type of adhesive that stuck and unstuck, and he was about to throw it away because he couldn't think of a use for it. Things went very well for him using this adhesive, because it stuck to the pieces of paper that marked the pages where the selected hymns were printed. "Eureka!" he said. "This could be a product for the company to develop!" He showed it to the manager but he replied that he couldn't see a future for it because of the high production cost. However, he felt sure that it would get results, and could help other people. He kept insisting until the manager finally agreed to try it in the company to observe the results, despite his own skepticism about the costs. The company agreed to market the product, and guess what, it was a resounding success worldwide. What 3M developed were the famous *Post-It Notes*, the little pieces of paper we use every day to write notes on and stick them up so we don't forget.

As a result, the company developed a incentives plan for collaborators who came up with innovative ideas. A strategy was implemented inside the company using idea boxes, among other things. This caused synergy and even today it produces hundreds of new products each year. The creators of innovative ideas that are well accepted in the market and produce financial benefits for the company, receive a royalty.

As a result of this story 3M changed, and a radical transformation took place in the company. It went from producing a few items to becoming a global company that is among the 500 biggest in the world, with 67,000 employees and 132 plants. What allowed this change was the vision of one of its collaborators and the flexibility of his manager vis-à-vis a market need. It started with an idea, a new strategy, and a new plan to make and remake the ladder.

-I'm convinced- interrupted Charlie, and he started drawing his ladder.

Always remember that we are what we do repeatedly, so excellence means persevering with our objectives until they become habits, and then a reality.

-Thank you! Thank you very much!- said Charlie warmly, as he said good bye.

Before he left, Andrew asked: -Did you notice that theory is completely different from reality?

-Totally!- replied Charlie.

-Theory is just a guide- explained Andrew. -It will never be reality. Reality is changeable and continuous, and it always prevails over theory. Moreover, that is how new ideas are created. Only in real life can you apply your knowledge, but it should not be rigid.

You cannot apply a theory strictly. You always have to create a new formula.

Companies that always follow this practice will be ahead of their competitors. However, there are some ingredients in the formula that are changeless. They are principles and they cannot be changed.

-What principles?- asked Charlie.

X

VALUES ALIGNED WITH PRINCIPLES

-A few months ago I met a ship's captain and he told me a strange story- Andrew began. He told me that one day he was sailing in the Pacific Ocean when one of his sailors alerted him, saying that there was a ship dead ahead in the distance. It was nighttime and a strong storm was brewing. Captain Bruno Manchester asked the sailor to contact the other ship and ask it to change course. "This is seaman Domenech of the Battleship Rebell. Please turn to port as our ship is heading straight toward you," radioed the sailor. The signal was received and answered immediately: "Seaman Bodenmann here. It is you who should change course."

Furious, Domenech went to tell Manchester what had happened: "Captain, the other ship says that we are the ones who should change course." "What!" "What does this mean?" demanded Manchester indignantly, and he ordered the sailor: "Tell them that we are the famous Battleship Rebell under the command of Captain Bruno Manchester. Tell them that we are armed, and if they don't want problems they had better change course." The sailor obeyed immediately and radioed: "This is seaman Domenech again speaking on behalf of Captain Bruno Manchester. We are armed and we order you to change course." "This is seaman Bodenmann" came the reply. "It is urgent that you change course." After hearing the message, the sailor was very worried about giving the news to Manchester: "Captain, again they answered that we are the ones who have to change course." "I can't believe this" shouted the captain. I'm going to have to do this myself." He ran to the radio to respond to what seemed to him to be an enormous insult. "This is Captain Bruno Manchester of the Battleship Rebell, the most famous and dangerous in the navy. I order you to change course at once. Otherwise I will sink you. I await your immediate answer…" Straight away an answer came back from the other side: "This is seaman Bodenmann, Captain Manchester. You are the ones who have to change course. We are a lighthouse."

Andrew finished the story and Charlie was flabbergasted.

-Lighthouses are principles- explained Andrew. You can never move them from where they are. You can collide with them again and again, but they always remain unchanged. They are like the laws of nature. The law of gravity, for example, says that everything that goes up must come down, so if you jump of a ten-story building, all that will be left of you will be a pile of dust.

That is why the values you chose to guide your life should be aligned to principles. Otherwise you will collide with them.

-Remember that important people in history have used this philosophy successfully, like Gandhi in his struggle to free India without bloodshed. He used peace as his most powerful tool and won. Others, like Hitler, had values such as loyalty to your ideals, but those ideals were not aligned with principles, so they collided with one of the most important, respect for the life and freedom of innocent people. That was why he lost.

-It is extremely important to understand that principles are the source of values, and always ensure that they are aligned.

PRINCIPLES SHOULD BE THE SOURCE OF VALUES.

VALUES	PRINCIPLES
Responsibility toward work and commitments undertaken.	Respect for our fellow beings (their lives, property, liberty, etc.).
Unequivocal excellence in all aspects of the company.	Seeking justice in the light of natural reason.
Continuous innovation based on technology.	Truthfulness at all times.
Safeguarding creativity.	Transparency.
Careful attention to coherence and details.	Doing something for others, especially for those in the greatest need.
To be pioneers, to do the impossible and not follow the rest.	Self-sustainability.
Loyalty toward the company.	Subsidiarity (teaching someone how to fish, not just giving him a fish).
Honesty toward fellow-employees.	

Always try to negotiate so that both sides are satisfied with the agreements and results.

Get completely involved in the whole negotiation process, and let values and principles be your guide. The other side will see how meticulous and professional you are.

Let your actions show comprehension so that others can understand your side.

XI

CHANGING MANAGERS OR MANAGING CHANGE

Charlie went to work the next morning. As he entered the building he felt like a new person, full of energy and a desire to do things right. As he walked through the lobby, he even saw a picture hanging on the main wall that he hadn't noticed before. It contained a message that moved him: "You should always remember that a wise man lives in action. He does not think about acting, nor does he think about how the action will take place, or what the results will be. A wise man chooses a path and follows it with all his passion."

Strengthened by that message he summoned the elevator, but then he realized it was off. He imagined that the electricity had been cut off for lack of payment, but he didn't mind. There was a different Charlie since the meeting with his guru. He quickly climbed the stairs to his office and began to put all his knowledge into practice. The first thing he did was review all the papers on his desk to see what was really useful. He called the cleaning department and told them to clean the building thoroughly, and when everything was in order he began to call his collaborators one by one.

Mind came in with haughty air. He didn't take off his fine straw hat, and of course, his cigar was lit.

-Tell me Charlie, what do you want?- Mind asked.

-The first thing you are going to do- replied Charlie, -is to get rid of that cigar. Then you are going to take off your hat and start treating me with respect. You decide how to do it, but I want it to start now.

Seeing Charlie so firm and determined, Mind decided to beat around the bush:

-It looks like you talked to the boss.

Charlie cut him off before Mind could say any more.

-Yes, I talked to Andrew, and he gave me enough information to start reorganizing the company. We are going to implement a complete reengineering project and I am only going to keep collaborators who want to be on my side. So I want to know. What you are going to do- asked Charlie sharply.

Mind was surprised by these words and changed his tune:

-Yes boss, you can count on me- he replied.

-Wonderful!- exclaimed Charlie. —I knew I could count on you. As I said, we are going to clean house and set some goals. I know very well what your weaknesses are and we are going to turn them into strengths. First of all I want you to be clear. Don't speak to me ambiguously, and don't bring me gossip or information that is not real. I don't need you to start telling me about people who are not present and can't defend themselves. I want you to bring all the tools necessary for achieving the goals. We have to define all the priorities that we need to review and set each day, until we start meeting our objectives. Furthermore, I want you to instill this new order and discipline into all the staff. Tell them they can come to me any time they like, but they should always be well prepared with solid arguments and good judgment so that it will contribute to the company. I want you to lead this strategic plan and help implement the new company rules. I will be here whenever you need my support.

Strengthened and with new determination, Mind thanked his rejuvenated boss and left the office with a warm good-bye.

Without much delay, since Mind had already told him about Charlie's thoughts, Body appeared, completely surprised and curious about his coworker's new attitude.

-Hi Charlie- said the fat man with a sandwich in one hand and a soda in the other, while chewing a mouthful of his delicious food.

-Good morning Body- Charlie replied. -Would you stop eating and get rid of that soda immediately, please.

Hearing his boss speak so bluntly, he had no alternative but to abandon his pleasures.

-Look Body- Charlie continued. —Today is a new day for you, if you agree, of course.

-I don't understand, boss,- replied Body timidly. —What do you mean, if I agree?

-It was very clear to me from what you said yesterday that our entire system is slow, and it's a miracle if information gets to its destination. As of today, this is going to change. Mind and I have contacted Andrew about a new investment that will allow us to finance the operation and solve some problems. The money will be repaid in due time with interest. You and I are going to design a program to make the necessary changes in the organizational system. We are going to work quickly, get fast Internet, and improve our product distribution system to ensure that our customers receive their orders complete and on time. We will work day and night to find our bottlenecks and eliminate them one by one. I want us to have a global vision of where our company is going as a result of these necessary corrections and improvements. I also want you to start exercising and come up to the gym with me every day, and start eating a healthy diet that includes all the food groups in a balanced manner. We are going to make a contract so that we each do our part and work as a team to get out of this quagmire as soon as possible.

Inspired, Body remembered that when he was thin, he was more efficient and fast, and was also a lot more attractive to the opposite sex. He decided to bring a photograph of that time for encouragement, and accepted Charlie's proposal.

Body left the room much faster than usual, despite his size. He had the necessary motivation to start making positive changes, and that was what made him more agile.

It appeared that Mind had understood the message well, because Memories was outside waiting for his corpulent colleague to finish his meeting. With a quick greeting he came into the office and began reminding his boss about a very painful memory. It was so painful that Charlie was almost overcome, despite how motivated he was. Memories suggested that at least once in his life one of his best friends must have been disloyal to him and broken a promise, even after giving his word about something important they had agreed.

-This is going to make me lose heart- though Charlie. It is only an experience and will serve as feedback.

He remembered Andrew's words about feedback from difficult situations that had occurred in the past, and began to tighten the screws on his visitor.

-Mr. Memories- he said. -We are going to make a deal, type it up, and sign it. But more than that, we are going to fulfill it. The satisfaction we will obtain from achieving this will be unique, like every moment in life and each life that is born each day are unique. Every morning when you wake up, I want you to ask yourself these two questions:

1.- How many days do I have today? This question will help you to pay attention to the only day you have to fulfill your goals. That day is today. Although this may seem a bit dramatic, it is the truth, because tomorrow we may not be in this world.

2.- Does what I am doing really fulfill me and satisfy me? If the answer to that question during several days is NO, I will propose a change to what I really want.

The deal is that you are going to bring me all the positive memories I have lived, like when I graduated from the university, or when I won the soccer championship for my high school after a lot of effort. When I moved up a belt in karate, or when I solved that problem in high school and managed to pass the year, or when I got a promotion and was congratulated by my boss and coworkers for the creative idea I implemented to improve productivity. We're going to bring all these positive memories for our coworkers too, and link them together to start creating a new company. It will be a leader in all its fields and everybody will want to work here and help it become stronger financially. However, we are going to proceed step by step, and always bear in mind a very important phrase:

"To travel far you need to go slowly, and to be successful you have to be steadfast."

Memories left Charlie's office with contagious enthusiasm. One the way out he ran into Feelings, waiting for his turn. Very nervous and surprised by the enthusiasm of his coworkers, he entered silently.

-Very good, Feelings- Charlie began. –The time for change has arrived, and it's a unique moment in your life. You are going to use it to make a choice that will bring you balance and tranquility, and make us strong and dynamic. With your support on the management team, we will become the best company in our field. You will be in charge of bringing positive feelings and enthusiasm, and making sure that all this joy and optimism permeates the language of our people. You are going to promote daily self-motivation so that they can achieve their personal and company goals. They will smile when they discover the change in the surroundings where they work and in their lives, and they will recover their feelings and their vision. They will understand clearly what they want and what they need to be happy, and will be able to differentiate between these two concepts. That will be an antidote for any negative thought that tries to intrude. They will not forget that only by being happy and satisfying their basic needs can they feel fulfilled and achieve their dreams. Finally, Feelings, fill us all with a spirit of gratitude for everything that happens to us, the day we are living in, our families, our friends, and the fact that we can create new things every day. Use your wisdom. You can do it.

Now, Feelings, I want you to please call your three coworkers so that I can tell them what I think about success.

With his four subordinates present, Charlie began to speak:

"I personally believe that success is not financial. I believe that a person is not a success just because his business deals go well, or he does well professionally, or he gets an A in school. I believe that those are the least important. What really counts is to have your feet on the ground and care for your family and friends. Appreciate things that have true value, not material or physical value. Success is not what many people think. It is not related to the academic degrees you have or the school you went to. It is not the size of your house or how many cars you have. It does not matter whether you are the boss or the subordinate, or if you belong to social clubs. It is not the power you have or whether you are a good manager or a good talker or whether lights follow you as you talk. It is not the clothes you wear or what you have embroidered on them, or if you put letters after your name that define your social status. It is not whether you are an entrepreneur, or speak several languages, or are attractive, young or old.

Success depends on how many people are happy to see you, how many people you love, and how many admire your sincerity and the simplicity of your spirit. It is whether they remember you when you are gone. It is how many people you help, how many you avoid hurting, and whether or not you harbor resentment in your heart. It is whether your triumphs include your dreams, and your achievements do not harm your fellow humans. It is about your inclusion with others, not your control over them. It is about whether you use your head as well as your heart, whether you are selfish or generous, whether you love nature and children, and whether you care about old people. It is about your kindness, your desire to serve, your ability to listen, and your courage about behavior. It is not about how many people follow you, but rather how many really love you. It is not about transmitting, but rather how many believe that you are really happy, or pretend to be. It is the balance of justice that leads to wealth and wellbeing. It is about your clear conscience, your unassailable dignity and your desire to be more, not to have more. THAT IS SUCCESS!!! AND I DESIRE IT FOR YOU IN ABUNDANCE.

The four colleagues were impressed by Charlie's striking words, and applauded enthusiastically. They then agreed to fulfill all the goals, and not lose their focus or neglect their vision and mission, and above all, to align their values with principles.

XII

THE FORMULA CONTINUES

As if he had been summoned by telepathy, Andrew appeared on the scene at that moment. He found them all in good spirits, and full of that element that no human being should be without: Positive Energy.

-I congratulate you- said Andrew. I see that you have finally found the leader you needed. You have formed a team. Saying that he asked Charlie to accompany him.

-Where are we going?- Charlie asked.

-After everything that has happened, I want you to come with me to visit the company you saw from your window- said Andrew. I am going to talk about the excellent results they have obtained, and next year I hope to give the same speech to the company you are managing.

Andrew began to speak to the staff of the other company:

-This is a message for all of you. You are like me, I believe in you, and I hope you fulfill all your dreams. I wagered a lot on you and you have won my appreciation, trust and admiration.

I only want to give you a brief message to transmit a little of what I really believe…

I believe more in scientists who use trial and error, than in people who rely only on cold statistics.
I believe in action more than in being a spectator.
I believe in a man who has the courage to face change.

I believe that sometimes we have to be confused in order to be able to learn more, investigate and grow.

I believe in people who can expand their horizons quickly and not stick with outmoded patterns.

I believe in knowledge, but I also believe that it can inflate the ego if we don't use it for the benefit of others. It is better to know that we know nothing in order to learn more, to know how to learn, and to learn always.

I believe in each of you because if you did not exist, there would be no reason for anything that exists. Remember that there will always be two paths: the path of the world, and the path of love. If you choose the path of the world you will not have love, but if you choose the path of love, with it you can conquer the world.

THE END

(Or does the learning start over?)

ANNEX

YOUR OWN LADDER OF SUCCESS

Start your own ladder of success:

Ladder of Success of: ………………………………………………………………..

The Ladder of Success

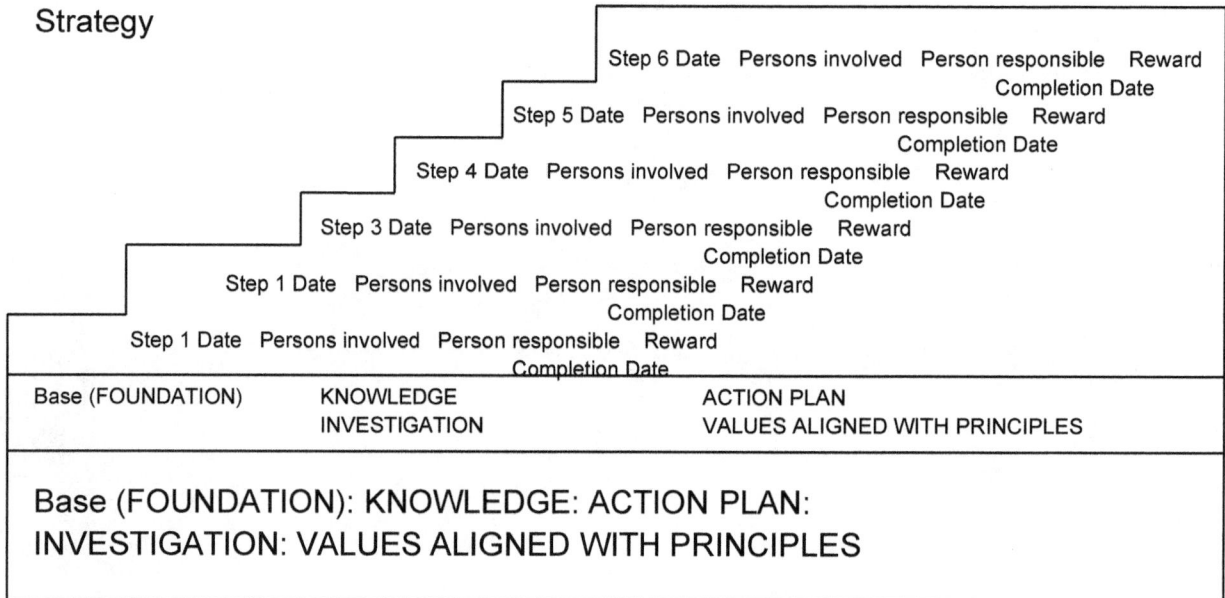

	Image of the desired future

Strategy

Step 6 Date   Persons involved   Person responsible   Reward
Completion Date

Step 5 Date   Persons involved   Person responsible   Reward
Completion Date

Step 4 Date   Persons involved   Person responsible   Reward
Completion Date

Step 3 Date   Persons involved   Person responsible   Reward
Completion Date

Step 1 Date   Persons involved   Person responsible   Reward
Completion Date

Step 1 Date   Persons involved   Person responsible   Reward
Completion Date

Base (FOUNDATION)	KNOWLEDGE INVESTIGATION	ACTION PLAN VALUES ALIGNED WITH PRINCIPLES

Base (FOUNDATION): KNOWLEDGE: ACTION PLAN:
INVESTIGATION: VALUES ALIGNED WITH PRINCIPLES